PHILIPPIANS

Running the Race

Group Directory

Pass this Directory around and have your Group Members
fill in their names and phone numbers

Name   **Phone**

_____   _____

_____   _____

_____   _____

_____   _____

_____   _____

_____   _____

_____   _____

_____   _____

_____   _____

_____   _____

_____   _____

_____   _____

_____   _____

_____   _____

_____   _____

_____   _____

PHILIPPIANS

Running the Race

EDITING AND PRODUCTION TEAM:
James F. Couch, Jr., Lyman Coleman, Sharon Penington, Mike Shepherd,
Christopher Werner, Matthew Lockhart, Mary Chatfield, Richard Peace,
Andrew Sloan, Erika Tiepel, Keith Madsen, Cathy Tardif, Scott Lee

NASHVILLE, TENNESSEE

Running the Race: A Study of Endurance Based on Philippians
© 1988, 1998, 2003 Serendipity House
Reprinted July 2004

Published by Serendipity House Publishers
Nashville, Tennessee

ISBN: 1-5749-4324-3

Dewey Decimal Classification: 227.6
Subject Headings:
BIBLE. N.T. PHILIPPIANS—STUDY AND TEACHING \ CHRISTIAN LIFE

Unless otherwise indicated, all Scripture quotations are taken from the
Holman Christian Standard Bible®,
Copyright © 1999, 2000, 2002, 2003 by Holman Bible Publishers. Used by permission.

To purchase additional copies of this resource or other studies:
ORDER ONLINE at www.SerendipityHouse.com
WRITE Serendipity House, 117 10th Avenue North, Nashville, TN 37234
FAX (615) 277-8181
PHONE (800) 525-9563

1-800-525-9563
www.SerendipityHouse.com

Printed in the United States of America
10 09 08 07 06 05 04   2 3 4 5 6 7 8 9 10

Table of Contents

Core Values

Community: The purpose of this curriculum is to build community within the body of believers around Jesus Christ.

Group Process: To build community, the curriculum must be designed to take a group through a step-by-step process of sharing your story with one another.

Interactive Bible Study: To share your "story," the approach to Scripture in the curriculum needs to be open-ended and right brain—to "level the playing field" and encourage everyone to share.

Developmental Stages: To provide a healthy program throughout the four stages of the life cycle of a group, the curriculum needs to offer courses on three levels of commitment: (1) Beginner Level—low-level entry, high structure, to level the playing field; (2) Growth Level—deeper Bible study, flexible structure, to encourage group accountability; (3) Discipleship Level—in-depth Bible study, open structure, to move the group into high gear.

Target Audiences: To build community throughout the culture of the church, the curriculum needs to be flexible, adaptable and transferable into the structure of the average church.

Mission: To expand the Kingdom of God one person at a time by filling the "empty chair." (We add an extra chair to each group session to remind us of our mission.)

Introduction

Each healthy small group will move through various stages as it matures.

Growth Stage: Here the group begins to care for one another as it learns to apply what they learn through Bible study, worship and prayer.

Develop Stage: The inductive Bible study deepens while the group members discover and develop gifts and skills. The group explores ways to invite their neighbors and coworkers to group meetings.

Birth Stage: This is the time in which group members form relationships and begin to develop community. The group will spend more time in ice-breaker exercises, relational Bible study and covenant building.

Multiply Stage: The group begins the multiplication process. Members pray about their involvement in new groups. The "new" groups begin the life cycle again with the Birth Stage.

Subgrouping: If you have nine or more people at a meeting, Serendipity recommends you divide into subgroups of 3–6 for the Bible study. Ask one person to be the leader of each subgroup and to follow the directions for the Bible study. After 30 minutes, the Group Leader will call "time" and ask all subgroups to come together for the Caring Time.

Each group meeting should include all parts of the "three-part agenda."

Ice-Breaker: Fun, history-giving questions are designed to warm the group and to build understanding about the other group members. You can choose to use all of the Ice-Breaker questions, especially if there is a new group member that will need help in feeling comfortable with the group.

One of the purposes of this book is to begin a group. Therefore, getting to know one another and bonding together are essential to the success of this course. The goal is to get acquainted during the Ice-Breaker part of each group session.

Bible Study: The heart of each meeting is the reading and examination of the Bible. The questions are open, discover questions that lead to further inquiry. Reference notes are provided to give everyone a "level playing field." The emphasis is on understanding what the Bible says and applying the truth to real life. The questions for each session build. There is always at least one "going deeper" question provided. You should always leave time for the last of the "questions for interaction." Should you choose, you can use the optional "going deeper" question to satisfy the desire for the challenging questions in groups that have been together for a while.

To help bond together as a group, it is important for everyone to participate in the Bible Study. There are no right or wrong answers to the questions. The group members should strive to make all of the other group members feel comfortable during the Bible Study time. Because we all have differing levels of biblical knowledge, it is essential that we appreciate the personal context from which answers are given. We don't have to know much about Scripture to bring our own perspectives on the truths contained in the Scriptures. It is vital to keep encouraging all group members to share what they are observing as we work through these important Bible passages.

Caring Time: All study should point us to actions. Each session ends with prayer and direction in caring for the needs of the group members. You can choose between several questions. You should always pray for the "empty chair." Who do you know that could fill that void in your group?

Small groups help the larger body of Christ in many ways: caring for individuals, holding one another up in prayer, providing emotional support and in bringing new people into the body through filling the empty chair. Each week it is important to remember to pray for those who God would bring to fill your empty chair.

Sharing Your Story: These sessions are designed for members to share a little of their personal lives each time. Through a number of special techniques each member is encouraged to move from low risk, less personal sharing to higher risk responses. This helps develop the sense of community and facilitates caregiving.

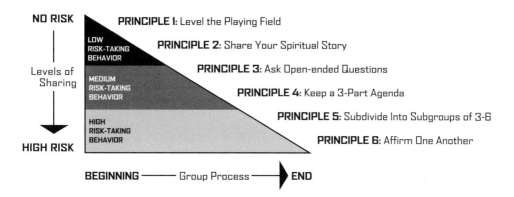

Group Covenant: A group covenant is a "contract" that spells out your expectations and the ground rules for your group. It's very important that your group discuss these issues—preferably as part of the first session.

GROUND RULES:

- Priority: While you are in the group, you give the group meeting priority.

- Participation: Everyone participates and no one dominates.

- Respect: Everyone is given the right to their own opinion and all questions are encouraged and respected.

- Confidentiality: Anything that is said in the meeting is never repeated outside the meeting.

- Empty Chair: The group stays open to new people at every meeting.

- Support: Permission is given to call upon each other in time of need—even in the middle of the night.

- Advice Giving: Unsolicited advice is not allowed.

- Mission: We agree to do everything in our power to start a new group as our mission.

ISSUES:

- The time and place this group is going to meet is_____

- Refreshments are _____ responsibility.

- Child care is _____ responsibility.

Our Small Group Covenant

1. The facilitator for this group is _____.

2. The apprentice facilitator this group is _____.

3. This group will meet from _____ to _____ on _____.

4. This group will normally meet at _____.

5. Childcare will be arranged by _____.

6. Refreshments will be coordinated by _____.

7. Our primary purpose for meeting is _____.

8. Our secondary purpose for meeting is _____.

9. We all agree to follow the ground rules listed below:

   a. This meeting will be given priority in our schedules.

   b. Everyone will participate in each meeting and no one will dominate a meeting.

   c. Each has a right to one's own opinion and all questions will be respected.

   d. Everything that is said in group meetings is never to be repeated outside of the meeting.

   e. This group will be open to new people at every meeting.

   f. Permission is given for all to call on each other in time of need.

   g. Unsolicited advice is not allowed.

   h. We agree to fill the empty chair and work toward starting new groups.

10. We are to hold one another accountable to meet any commitments mutually agreed upon by this group.

I agree to all of the above _____ date _____

Individual and Group Needs Survey

Check the types of studies that you find most interesting:

❑ Issues about spiritual development, such as learning to love like God does or knowing God's will.

❑ Studying about the life and message of Jesus Christ.

❑ Issues about personal development, such as managing stress or understanding the stages of growth in marriage.

❑ Learning about the major truths of the Christian faith.

❑ Studying the teaching of the Apostle Paul.

❑ Working through specific areas of personal struggle, such as coping with teenagers or recovering from divorce.

❑ Learning about the books of the New Testament other than the Gospels and Epistles of Paul.

Rank the following factor in order of importance to you with 1 being the highest and five being the lowest:

_____ The passage of Scripture that is being studied.

_____ The topic or issue that is being discussed.

_____ The affinity of group members (age, vocation, interest).

_____ The mission of the group (service projects, evangelism, starting groups).

_____ Personal encouragement.

Rank the following spiritual development needs in order of interest to you with 1 being the highest and 5 being the lowest:

_____ Learning how to become a follower of Christ.

_____ Gaining a basic understanding of the truths of the faith.

_____ Improving my disciplines of devotion, prayer, reading Scripture.

_____ Gaining a better knowledge of what is in the Bible.

_____ Applying the truths of Scripture to my life.

Of the various studies listed below check the appropriate boxes to indicate:

P - if you would be interested in studying this for your **personal needs**

G - if you think it would be helpful for your **group**

F - if **friends** that are not in the group would come to a group studying this subject

Growing in Christ Series (7-week studies)	P	G	F
Keeping Your Cool: Dealing with Stress	❑	❑	❑
Personal Audit: Assessing Your life	❑	❑	❑
Seasons of Growth: Stages of Marriage	❑	❑	❑
Checking Your Moral Compass: Personal Morals	❑	❑	❑
Women of Faith (8 weeks)	❑	❑	❑
Men of Faith	❑	❑	❑
Being Single and the Spiritual Quest	❑	❑	❑

Foundations of the Faith (7-week studies)	P	G	F
Knowing Jesus	❑	❑	❑
Foundational Truths	❑	❑	❑
God and the Journey to Truth	❑	❑	❑
The Christian in the Postmodern World	❑	❑	❑

Fellowship Church Series (6-week studies)	P	G	F
Wired for Worship (worship as a lifestyle)	❑	❑	❑
X-Trials: Takin' Life to the X-treme (James)	❑	❑	❑
Virtuous Reality: The Relationships of David	❑	❑	❑
Praying for Keeps (life of prayer)	❑	❑	❑
Character Tour (developing godly character)	❑	❑	❑

Becoming a Disciple (7-week studies)	P	G	F
Discovering God's Will	❑	❑	❑
Time for a Checkup	❑	❑	❑
Learning to Love	❑	❑	❑
Making Great Kids	❑	❑	❑
Becoming Small-Group Leaders	❑	❑	❑

Understanding the Savior (13-week studies)	P	G	F
Jesus, the Early Years (Mark 1 – 8)	❑	❑	❑
Jesus, the Final Days (Mark 9 – 16)	❑	❑	❑
John: God in the Flesh (John 1 – 11)	❑	❑	❑
John: The Passion of the Son (John 12 – 21)	❑	❑	❑
The Life of Christ	❑	❑	❑
Sermon on the Mount: Jesus, the Teacher	❑	❑	❑
The Parables of Jesus	❑	❑	❑
The Miracles of Jesus	❑	❑	❑

The Message of Paul	P	G	F
Who We Really Are: Romans 1 – 7 (13 weeks)	❑	❑	❑
Being a Part of God's Plan: Romans 8 – 16 (13 weeks)	❑	❑	❑
Taking on Tough Issues: 1 Corinthians (13 weeks)	❑	❑	❑
Living by Grace: Galatians (13 weeks)	❑	❑	❑
Together in Christ: Ephesians (12 weeks)	❑	❑	❑
Running the Race: Philippians (7 weeks)	❑	❑	❑
Passing the Torch: 1 & 2 Timothy (13 weeks)	❑	❑	❑

Men of Purpose Series (13-week studies geared to men)	P	G	F
Overcoming Adversity: Insights into the Life of Joseph	❑	❑	❑
Fearless Leadership: Insights into the Life of Joshua	❑	❑	❑
Unwavering Tenacity: Insights into the Life of Elijah	❑	❑	❑
Shoulder to Shoulder: Insights into the Life of the Apostles	❑	❑	❑

Words of Faith	P	G	F
The Church on Fire: Acts 1 – 14 (13 weeks)	❏	❏	❏
The Irrepressible Witness: Acts 15 – 28 (13 weeks)	❏	❏	❏
The True Messiah: Hebrews (13 weeks)	❏	❏	❏
Faith at Work: James (12 weeks)	❏	❏	❏
Staying the Course: 1 Peter (10 weeks)	❏	❏	❏
Walking in the Light: 1 John (11 weeks)	❏	❏	❏
The End of Time: Revelation 1 – 12 (13 weeks)	❏	❏	❏
The New Jerusalem: Revelation 13 – 22 (13 weeks)	❏	❏	❏

301 Bible Studies with Home Work Assignments (13-week studies)	P	G	F
Life of Christ: Behold the Man	❏	❏	❏
Sermon on the Mount: Examining Your Life	❏	❏	❏
Parables: Virtual Reality	❏	❏	❏
Miracles: Signs and Wonders	❏	❏	❏
Ephesians: Our Riches in Christ	❏	❏	❏
Philippians: Joy under Stress	❏	❏	❏
James: Walking the Talk	❏	❏	❏
1 John: The Test of Faith	❏	❏	❏

Life Connections Series (Unique series blends master-teacher larger group format with effective small-group encounters; 13-week studies)

	P	G	F
Essential Truth: Knowing Christ Personally	❏	❏	❏
Vital Pursuits: Developing My Spiritual Life	❏	❏	❏
Authentic Relationships: Being Real in an Artificial World	❏	❏	❏
Unique Design: Connecting with the Christian Community	❏	❏	❏
Acts: Model for Today's Church	❏	❏	❏
Critical Decisions: Surviving in Today's World	❏	❏	❏
Colossians: Navigating Successfully Through Cultural Chaos	❏	❏	❏
Intentional Choices: Discovering Contentment in Stressful Times	❏	❏	❏
Unleashed Influence: Power of servant Leadership	❏	❏	❏

Felt Need Series (7-week studies)	P	G	F
Stress Management: Finding the Balance	❏	❏	❏
12 Steps: The Path to Wholeness	❏	❏	❏
Divorce Recovery: Picking Up the Pieces	❏	❏	❏
Parenting Adolescents: Easing the Way to Adulthood	❏	❏	❏
Blended Families: Yours, Mine, Ours	❏	❏	❏
Healthy Relationships: Living Within Defined Boundaries	❏	❏	❏
Marriage Enrichment: Making a Good Marriage Better	❏	❏	❏

For the latest studies visit www.SerendipityHouse.com or call 1-800-525-9563.

A Note of Thanks

Scripture Philippians 1:1–11

Philippians is a letter of joy. Joy permeates its pages from start to finish. And yet this is not joy forged out of privilege and abundance. It is not the joy of people who have no problems to face. This is joy in the midst of hard situations. Paul is writing from prison, and he faces the very real possibility of execution. The Philippian church is confronted with internal dissension and with false teachers who would seduce it away from the Gospel.

How can you be joyful in that kind of world? How can you call others to joy when you are in prison? The typical Christian today does not know how to answer these questions, because joy is thought to be what comes with prosperity and success. Joy is what happens when your church is growing and when its influence is spreading in the community. Joy is the lack of pressure and hardship. Philippians is a letter that helps us to address these questions and experience a joy that is with us in the ups and downs of life.

The letter was written by Paul to the Christians in Philippi, a city in the Roman province of Macedonia (modern Greece), eight miles from the Mediterranean Sea in a fertile area known for its freshwater springs and gold mines. Philip II, the king of Macedonia, founded Philippi around 360 B.C. so that he could mine its gold in order to finance his army. The city was named for Philip, the father of Alexander the Great. As a result of Rome's military conquests, Philippi came under Roman rule in 168 B.C. After a while it became a Roman colony. This meant that to live in Philippi was like living in Rome itself. One had all the rights and privileges accorded those in the capital. At the time of Paul, the citizens of Philippi, who were mostly Romans (though there were some Greeks and a few Jews), were very proud of their city and its special tie to Rome.

The church at Philippi was founded during Paul's second missionary journey. Paul had a vision in which a "man from Macedonia" beckoned him to "Come over ... and help us" (Acts 16:9). Paul did just that. He sailed almost immediately from Asia, and after two days arrived at the Macedonian seaport of Neapolis. Paul and his party then pressed on to the city of Philippi to begin work. Paul joined a group of women who met on the Sabbath by the banks of the river Gangites to recite prayers. There he met Lydia, a successful merchant whose business was trading in the purple cloth

> *Welcome to this study of the letter by Paul to the Philippians. Together we will look at this positive letter and its call to rejoice even in the midst of hard times. We will find in God and this supportive community the resources we need to let its teachings change our lives.*

for which her hometown of Thyatira was famous. She listened to Paul's message and was converted along with her whole household. They were the first European Christians. Lydia was not Jewish, but was a "God-fearer," that is, a Gentile who participated in Jewish worship without becoming a proselyte. Her house became the center of missionary activity in Philippi.

Paul soon ran into trouble in Philippi, however. He cast out a demon from a fortune-telling slave girl, and she promptly lost her ability to predict the future. This outraged her owners, who saw that they stood to lose a great deal of money now that the girl was out from under the bondage of the demon. So they had Paul and Silas thrown in jail. After an earthquake during the night and their jailer, with his whole household being saved, the magistrates discovered that Paul and Silas were Roman citizens. The magistrates order that they be released and told Paul and Silas to leave the city. Thus they left Philippi, leaving behind them the first European church.

This church was always special to Paul, and he to it. Years later there was still a warm feeling of mutual care and concern between Paul and the Philippians, so much so that in his epistles Paul calls them his "joy and crown" (4:1).

Paul probably wrote this letter to the church that was his "joy and crown" when he was in Rome under house arrest, awaiting trial, some time after A.D. 60. Paul was in prison when Epaphroditus, an old friend from Philippi, arrived bearing a gift from the church. Paul sent Epaphroditus back to Philippi along with a letter thanking them for their gift and all they meant to him. This also enabled Paul to inform them that he hoped to send Timothy to see them soon, and that he himself would come when he was released from prison.

 Ice-Breaker Connect With Your Group (15 minutes)

The relationships we have with family members and friends are one of the joys that get us through our journey in life. Today we are beginning our journey through Philippians, and one thing we will see is the love Paul had for the friends he made as he spread the Gospel. Take turns sharing how you feel about those special relationships in your life.

1. If you could pick just one person from your childhood to thank God for, other than those in your immediate family, who would it be? What would you especially thank God for in this person?

2. How well do you communicate with people you care about who are away from you? Rate yourself on a scale of 1 ("I'm so bad that my loved ones think I'm dead") to 10 ("I make phone calls to discuss the e-mails I wrote explaining what I said in my last letter").

3. If you could send a letter or e-mail to someone with whom you grew up, who would you want to send it to, and what would you say?

Bible Study Read Scripture and Discuss (30 minutes)

Paul was a prolific letter writer, and his letters almost always started out the same way—he thanked God for the people to whom he was writing. His letter to the Philippians is perhaps the best example of this because this church held such a special place in his heart. Looking at what he wrote reminds us of how important it is to affirm the people we care about and the relationship we have with them. Read Philippians 1:1–11 and note how Paul prays for the Philippians.

Leader
Select a member of the group ahead of time to read aloud the Scripture passage. Then discuss the Questions for Interaction, dividing into subgroups of three to six. Be sure to save time at the end for the Caring Time.

A Note of Thanks

1 Paul and Timothy, slaves of Christ Jesus:
To all the saints in Christ Jesus who are in Philippi, including the overseers and deacons.
²Grace to you and peace from God our Father and the Lord Jesus Christ.

³I give thanks to my God for every remembrance of you, ⁴always praying with joy for all of you in my every prayer, ⁵because of your partnership in the gospel from the first day until now. ⁶I am sure of this, that He who started a good work in you will carry it on to completion until the day of Christ Jesus. ⁷It is right for me to think this way about all of you, because I have you in my heart, and you are all partners with me in grace, both in my imprisonment and in the defense and establishment of the gospel. ⁸For God is my witness, how I deeply miss all of you with the affection of Christ Jesus. ⁹And I pray this: that your love will keep on growing in knowledge and every kind of discernment, ¹⁰so that you can determine what really matters and can be pure and blameless in the day of Christ, ¹¹filled with the fruit of righteousness that comes through Jesus Christ, to the glory and praise of God.

Philippians 1:1–11

Questions for Interaction

Leader
Refer to the Summary and Study Notes at the end of this section as needed. If 30 minutes is not enough time to answer all of the questions in this section, conclude the Bible Study by answering question 7.

1. What one word best describes your own perception of how Paul begins this letter?

   ○ Touching.
   ○ Mushy.
   ○ Personal.
   ○ Saccharin-sweet.
   ○ Uplifting.
   ○ Other _____.

2. Were someone from your past to write a letter like this to you, what would be your first reaction?

    ○ "What does this guy want from me?"
    ○ "Oh, I'm not that important—am I?"
    ○ "It's really nice of him to say that!"
    ○ "It's about time someone said these things."
    ○ Other _____.

3. Why does Paul take such care to begin this letter by telling the Philippians how much he thanks God for them? What effect do you think such an expression had on the church at Philippi?

4. How is God at work in a believer's life according to verses 6 and 9–11? How does this make you feel about uncertainties in your life?

5. On a scale of 1 (easy) to 10 (hard), how difficult is it for you to express your feelings like Paul did here?

6. Who was the "apostle Paul" in your spiritual life, the person who introduced you to Jesus Christ and cared about your spiritual growth?

7. If you could have a spiritual encourager like Paul write you a letter right now, what would you most need to hear from him or her?

    ○ Assurance that I am doing something right.
    ○ Assurance of the truth of the Gospel.
    ○ Assurance that God really is in control.
    ○ A vision for what God is calling me to do.
    ○ Other _____.

Going Deeper   If your group has time and/or wants a challenge, go on to this question.

8. How well is your church doing at showing the kind of affirming love that Paul shows here? What does the church need to do to be more positive in how it deals with people?

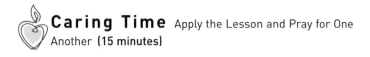

Caring Time Apply the Lesson and Pray for One Another (15 minutes)

Leader
Take some extra time in this first session to go over the group covenant found at the beginning of this book. At the close, pass around your books and have everyone sign the Group Directory. You, as leader, pray for the requests shared by the group.

This very important time is for each of you to express concern for other group members by praying for one another.

1. Agree on the group covenant and ground rules that are described in the introduction to this book.

2. What does this group need to be like for us to serve as encouragers to each other as Paul did? Pray for God to help this happen.

3. Share any other prayer requests and praises, and then close in prayer. Pray specifically for God to bring someone into your life next week to fill the empty chair.

NEXT WEEK *Today we looked at the positive spirit with which Paul opened this letter and what it says to us about being positive with each other. In the coming week, write a note of encouragement to your pastor or someone who has helped you spiritually. Next week we will consider the tough things Paul was going through, and how he saw them as serving to advance the Gospel.*

Summary: In a typical Greek letter, following the salutation, a prayer was offered on behalf of the recipients. Paul follows the custom here, as he does in most of his letters. Specifically, he thanks God for the long partnership he has had with the Philippians. He expresses his gratitude (vv. 3–6) and his affection for them (vv. 7–8). Then he tells them about his prayer for them.

1:1 *Timothy.* He had long been a companion of Paul. Timothy was with Paul when he visited Philippi for the first time and so was well known there. *slaves.* Paul lived a life of willing submission to the Lord, a point he will stress as he calls upon Christians to serve one another. *saints.* This designation is the general New Testament word for Christians, who, because of their union with Christ, have been "set apart" to serve God. *overseers and deacons.* The function of these individuals is not completely clear, except that they are leaders of some sort, quite possibly appointed by Paul.

1:2 *Grace to you and peace.* At this point in a Greek letter, the writer would say "rejoice." But here Paul wishes them "grace," which is a word that comes from the same Greek root as the secular greeting "rejoice." In a Hebrew letter, the writer would say "peace" (*shalom*). Paul links the two wishes together to form a distinctively Christian greeting.

1:3 *for every remembrance of you.* This is a difficult phrase to translate from the Greek. What it seems to mean is that Paul gave thanks for them regularly.

1:4 *with joy.* "Joy" is a theme that pervades Philippians. This is the first of some 14 times that Paul will use the word in this epistle. He mentions "joy" more often in this short epistle than in any of his other letters. It is interesting that his first reference to joy is in connection with prayer. *my every prayer.* This is not the usual Greek word for prayer. (That word is found in verse 9.) This is a word that carries the idea of "need" or "lack," and so came to mean intercessory prayer. Paul is praying that God will meet specific needs that he knows they have.

1:5 *because of your partnership.* Paul is grateful to God for the Philippians, because they have always stood by him in the work of the Gospel. The Greek word rendered here as "partnership" is the familiar word *koinonia*, translated elsewhere as "fellowship." It means, literally, "having something in common." It is a favorite word of Paul's. Of the 19 times it appears in the New Testament, he uses it 13 times. *in the gospel.* The Philippians were partners with Paul in spreading the Gospel. Specifically, they supported him financially in his ministry (2:25; 4:10–20). In addition, they worked with him to spread the Gospel (4:3); they prayed for him (1:19); and they contributed generously to the fund he raised in aid of the needy Christians in Jerusalem (2 Cor. 8:1–5). The word "Gospel" is another favorite of Paul's. He uses it 60 of the 76 times it appears in the New Testament. The Gospel is the Good News about what God has done in Christ Jesus to save men and women.

1:6 *I am sure of this.* Confidence is another of the underlying themes of Philippians. Paul makes it very clear what lies at the root of this confidence. It is not human accomplishment or ritual of any sort (3:3–4). This is confidence that springs out of faith in who God is and what he is doing. *the day of Christ Jesus.* This is the moment when Christ will return in glory and triumph to establish his kingdom on earth.

1:7 *because I have you in my heart.* The phrase could equally well be translated, as in the NEB, "because you hold me in such affection." In this case, the way Paul feels about the Philippians is based on their affection for him. Perhaps the phrase is intended to be ambiguous and to be read both ways, since there was a mutuality of affection between Paul and the Philippians. *in the defense and establishment of the gospel.* These are legal terms. The reference is to Paul's defense before the Roman court, in which he hopes to be able not only to vindicate himself and the Gospel from false charges, but to proclaim the Gospel in life-changing power to those in the courtroom. (See Acts 26 for an example of how Paul did this when he stood in court before Agrippa and Festus.)

1:8 *God is my witness.* In moments of deep feeling, Paul would sometimes invoke God to bear witness to the authenticity of these feelings (Rom. 1:9; 2 Cor. 11:11,31; 1 Thess. 2:5). *I deeply miss.* Yet another word that is characteristic of Paul. He uses it seven of the nine times it is found in the New Testament. This is a strong word and expresses the depth of Paul's feelings for them, his desire to be with them and wish to minister to them.

1:9 *And I pray this.* Paul's love for the Philippians leads him to pray on their behalf. What he prays is that they will overflow with love. He prays that this love will increase (i.e., that it will go on developing) through knowledge and discernment.

1:10 *so that you can determine what really matters.* The Philippians are confronted with competing ideologies as to what is true and how to live. They need "knowledge" and "discernment" in order to choose and follow that which is of God and what results in purity and blamelessness. The word translated as "determine" is used to describe the process of testing coins so as to distinguish between those that are real and those that are counterfeit.

Joyful in Imprisonment

Scripture Philippians 1:12–26

LAST WEEK *Last week we looked at the way Paul affirmed the Philippians, and we discussed our own need for spiritual encouragement. This week we will look at the joyful spirit that Paul had even though he was in prison and facing his own possible death. From this we will consider what real joy is.*

 Ice-Breaker Connect With Your Group (15 minutes)

"You're grounded!" When was the last time you heard or said those words? Most likely we heard those words a few times when we were teenagers. Take turns sharing your unique life experiences with trouble and its consequences.

1. When you were young, how often did you get "grounded" or "put on restriction"? What were you most frequently put on restriction for doing? Looking back, was your punishment fair?

2. Which of these "chains" did you feel most restricted by when you were a teen?

   ○ Strict parents.
   ○ Lack of money.
   ○ Negative attitudes toward young people.
   ○ Small-town attitudes.
   ○ A dangerous neighborhood.
   ○ My own shyness.
   ○ Other _____.

Leader
Begin the session with a word of prayer. Have your group members take turns sharing their responses to one, two or all three of the Ice-Breaker questions. Be sure that everyone gets a chance to participate.

3. Who do you remember trying to "stir up trouble" for you when you were in school? How did they do this, and how did you react?

 Bible Study Read Scripture and Discuss (30 minutes)

The apostle Paul was "put on restriction" by Rome for having preached the Gospel. Rather than simply going on and on about how unfair that was, he used his chains to advance the Gospel. He used the time in prison to write many of the letters we now have in the Bible, and he used the opportunity as well to witness to the ones who guarded him. All this he did in a spirit of joy, because he felt that if he had Christ then he had everything he needed. Read Philippians 1:12–26 and note how Paul lives to honor Christ.

Joyful in Imprisonment

[12]Now I want you to know, brothers, that what has happened to me has actually resulted in the advancement of the gospel, [13]so that it has become known throughout the whole imperial guard, and to everyone else, that my imprisonment is for Christ. [14]Most of the brothers in the Lord have gained confidence from my imprisonment and dare even more to speak the message fearlessly. [15]Some, to be sure, preach Christ out of envy and strife, but others out of good will. [16]These do so out of love, knowing that I am appointed for the defense of the gospel; [17]the others proclaim Christ out of rivalry, not sincerely, seeking to cause me trouble in my imprisonment. [18]What does it matter? Just that in every way, whether out of false motives or true, Christ is proclaimed. And in this I rejoice. Yes, and I will rejoice [19]because I know this will lead to my deliverance through your prayers and help from the Spirit of Jesus Christ. [20]My eager expectation and hope is that I will not be ashamed about anything, but that now as always, with all boldness, Christ will be highly honored in my body, whether by life or by death.

[21]For me, living is Christ and dying is gain. [22]Now if I live on in the flesh, this means fruitful work for me; and I don't know which one I should choose. [23]I am pressured by both. I have the desire to depart and be with Christ—which is far better— [24]but to remain in the flesh is more necessary for you. [25]Since I am persuaded of this, I know that I will remain and continue with all of you for your advancement and joy in the faith, [26]so that, because of me, your confidence may grow in Christ Jesus when I come to you again.

Philippians 1:12–26

1. What is the closest you have come as an adult to feeling like you were "imprisoned"?

   ○ Being in a restrictive job environment.
   ○ Being in a bad marriage.
   ○ Feeling enchained by guilt or bitterness.
   ○ Being chained to my past.
   ○ Other _____.

2. In what ways did Paul's imprisonment seem to advance the Gospel (vv. 13–14)?

3. What were some of the different motivations people had for preaching the Gospel? What is Paul's attitude about this? Why was he seemingly unconcerned about this issue of motivation?

4. What are some of the motivations you see people having for sharing the Gospel? Do any of these motivations concern you? What can you learn from Paul in this regard?

5. What did Paul mean by the phrase, "living is Christ, and dying is gain" (v. 21)? Which do you think he really most wanted to do, and why?

6. Paul tells the Philippians, "to remain in the flesh is more necessary for you" (v. 24). Who, beside yourself, really stands to benefit from you "remaining in the flesh"? What wider benefit is there for the kingdom of God for you to remain in this life instead of dying and going to be with God?

7. How have the negative things that have happened to you turned out in the end for your "deliverance" (v. 19)? How have you seen God working in this?

Going Deeper   If your group has time and/or wants a challenge, go on to this question.

8. How was Paul able to speak of rejoicing (v. 18b) and joy (v. 25) while in jail and in danger of losing his life? Having seen this, how would you define what "joy" is?

 **Caring Time** Apply the Lesson and Pray for One Another (15 minutes)

Come together for a time of sharing and prayer now, rejoicing in the promise that God will grant you "advancement and joy in the faith" (v. 25). Share your responses to the following questions and then support and encourage one another in prayer.

1. Where do you need to be encouraged to "speak the message fearlessly" (v. 14)? How can this group pray for you in that regard?

2. What are you going through right now that you find it hard to believe will turn out for your "deliverance" (v. 19)?

3. What reasons do you have to "rejoice" (v. 18)? Share these and rejoice with each other.

   P.S. *Add new group members to the Group Directory at the front of this book.*

Leader
Bring the group back together for the Caring Time. Begin by sharing responses to all three questions. Then share prayer requests and ask someone ahead of time to close in prayer.

NEXT WEEK *Today we looked at the tough things Paul was going through, and how he saw them as serving to advance the Gospel. We were also reminded how our true joy is found in Christ and not in our circumstances. In the coming week, ask the Holy Spirit to show you how you can use your circumstances to proclaim Christ to the world. Next week we will look at what Paul said about how the "worthy" living of the Philippians would similarly advance the Gospel.*

Summary: Paul began his letter in a traditional fashion with a salutation followed by thanksgiving and prayer. In verse 12 the letter proper begins, and the first thing Paul does is to provide his friends with news about himself. He reports on what has happened as a result of his imprisonment. He points to three positive outcomes, all involving the advance of the Gospel: (1) The Gospel is being noticed by all sorts of people who might otherwise not have heard it (v. 13); (2) the Christians in Rome have become bolder in their own proclamation (v. 14); and (3) even though some of the preaching that is going on springs from wrong motives, still the Gospel is getting out (vv. 15–18).

Paul's feelings go back and forth here. One moment he is confident that he would be released. The next, he is worried that he might bring shame on himself or on Christ. He longs to be with Christ, but he also wants to go on living so that he will be a source of joy for the Philippians. It is interesting to note that Paul is not at all reticent to express freely to his dear friends the full range of his emotions, including both his hopes and his fears.

1:12 *I want you to know.* This is a standard formula used in personal letters to indicate that the writer is now going to provide some personal information. Paul assures them that good is coming out of his imprisonment. He does not at this point say much directly about the actual conditions of his imprisonment or the progress that has been made in terms of his forthcoming trial (perhaps it was dangerous for him to put such information in a letter), but he does assure them that all this has had a positive effect on the spread of the Gospel. *brothers.* This is a generic term and means "brothers and sisters." By it Paul indicates the nature of his relationship with the Philippians. They are both a part of God's family. "Brothers" is a favorite term of Paul's. He uses it 133 times in his letters. *advancement.* A word used to describe an army that is moving forward despite obstacles. Paul's imprisonment could have had a negative effect on the spread of the Gospel. After all, here he was, the key evangelist, incarcerated and thus unable to get on with the preaching of the Gospel in the towns and the cities of the Roman world. Furthermore, his imprisonment could have cast a shadow over his message, with potential converts concluding that there was something criminal about what he was teaching. But the imprisonment had the opposite effect. People saw that this message was worth suffering for.

1:13 *imperial guard.* These men were the elite soldiers in the Roman army, the bodyguards of the emperor. Because Paul had been sent to Rome for a hearing before the emperor, they were given the task of guarding him. Paul's guards changed every four hours or so, and thus he got the chance to witness to a rotating coterie of soldiers from the key regiment in Rome. News of who he was and what he stood for apparently spread through the barracks and beyond into official circles. In 4:22, Paul will mention that some of those from Caesar's household had actually become Christians. *imprisonment.* Paul was not in a jail, but rather in a rented house where he was able to receive visitors, correspondence and gifts (4:18; Acts 28:16,30). He was, however, bound to a guard by a short chain that ran from his wrist to the guard's wrist. In such circumstances, it is not surprising that the guards got to know him and his Gospel.

1:14 Because of Paul's example, other Christians had become bolder in their own sharing of the Gospel, and so the message was being spread to even more people.

1:15 *Some.* Although "most" (v. 14) of the brothers and sisters have been inspired by Paul's example to be bolder in proclaiming the Gospel, "some" have used this imprisonment as the opportunity to advance their own honor, prestige or cause. However, Paul still considers these people to be "brothers." He may not like what they are doing, but he does not reject them as members of God's family. *envy and strife.* That which motivates these people is some kind of grudge or hostility directed against Paul. They did not like him and wanted to hurt him by their preaching. What lay behind this animosity is not clear. Perhaps they looked on Paul in disdain because he was in jail, seeing this as a judgment from God against him. Or maybe they were jealous of Paul's apostolic role and saw this as a golden opportunity to advance their own positions and prestige.

1:17 *rivalry.* The Greek word translated "rivalry" has an interesting history. It originally meant a "day laborer." It then came to mean someone who did "sordid work." It was also used in the political realm to describe a person who had a "partisan spirit." Eventually, it came to refer to a relentless careerist who would do almost anything to promote his or her own advancement.

1:18 *Christ is proclaimed.* The one fact that makes it possible for Paul to accept this situation—and in fact to find positive value in it—is that whatever else might be said about these wrongly motivated brothers and sisters, the message still centered on Christ. *And in this I rejoice.* This is an unexpected conclusion to Paul's report on his imprisonment. One might have expected an appeal that they pray for him in his difficult circumstances or that they work to get him released. This exclamation of joy is not how most people would sum up the experience of being in prison. But Paul has learned to see his circumstances in the light of God's plan; and so what matters is not how comfortable he

is but whether the Gospel is thriving—and since it is, Paul can rejoice! *Yes, and I will rejoice.* Here he prepares to give his second reason for rejoicing: He expects to be delivered from prison.

1:19 *I know.* How he "knows" that all this will result in his deliverance is not certain. Probably what he is referring to is a deep inner conviction that God will make right this situation. His confidence is based on two factors: their prayers and the work of the Holy Spirit.

1:20 *eager expectation.* This is a rare word, used only here and in Romans 8:19. Paul may even have coined this word himself. Why was Paul so eager to be released from prison and so filled with such expectation that he would be? Certainly the reasons had nothing to do with his ability to withstand suffering, although he might wish to be freed from it (2 Cor. 4:17), or that he feared death (vv. 21–23). Rather it was because release would demonstrate that he was innocent of any crime and especially prove that the Gospel he preached was not a subversive element in Roman society. *ashamed.* This is another rare word. In the New Testament, it is used only here and in 2 Cor. 10:8. But unlike "eager expectation," this word is used in other literature including the Old Testament. Depending on where one puts the "that,' this means that he is worried that he might disgrace either himself or the Gospel when he gets into court by not giving a proper defense. *boldness.* What Paul desires is the courage to speak boldly during his trial. This same word is used Ephesians 6:19–20 where Paul expresses the identical desire. *highly honored.* This word means, literally, to make something or someone large. When Paul uses this verb here he does not mean that his trial will succeed in making Christ greater, but rather it will serve to make Christ, who is great, known to a larger audience.

1:21 *living is Christ.* For Paul, his whole existence revolves around Christ. What he does, he does for Christ. *dying is gain.* Precisely because Paul's sole ambition is to be "for Christ," his life has not been at all easy. In 2 Corinthians 11:23–29 he recounts a litany of struggles, beatings, imprisonment, shipwreck, hunger, etc. Here in Philippians he mentions some of these hardships (1:29–30; 3:10; 4:14). Thus, with a load this heavy, it is not a surprise that death would seem attractive. But, for Paul, there is more to it than merely escape. Death is the door into the presence of Christ. Death is not so much escape from hardship as it is entrance into joy.

1:22 Paul does not know which path is best. "Dying is gain" but release from prison, which he anticipates, will give him the opportunity to do further missionary work. He may even be able to go to Spain as he had once planned (Rom. 15:24).

1:23 *to depart and be with Christ.* Death would be a gain for Paul since being with, in and for Christ meant everything to him. *which is far better.* Literally, "much rather better." So strong is Paul's desire to be with Christ that he uses a triple adverb as an emphatic superlative to describe his preference.

Right Living

Scripture Philippians 1:27–2:4

LAST WEEK *Last week we considered the joyful spirit that Paul had even though he was in prison and facing his own possible death. We were reminded how God can use even difficult circumstances to further his kingdom. This week we will see what Paul says about how the Christian should live and how that lifestyle is a witness to others of the Gospel.*

Ice-Breaker Connect With Your Group (15 minutes)

Leader
Welcome and introduce new group members. Be sure that everyone gets a chance to participate in the Ice-Breaker activity. Remember to stick closely to the three-part agenda and the time allowed for each segment.

Fear is an obstacle that can stand in the way of fulfilling God's plan for our lives. Paul knew this as he encouraged the Philippians not to be "frightened in any way by your opponents" (1:28). Take turns sharing how you have experienced fear and encouragement in your life.

1. What frightened you the most when you were in grade school?

   ○ The "monsters" under my bed or in the closet.
   ○ Bullies at school or in the neighborhood.
   ○ The possibility of failing in school, sports or some area of performance.
   ○ The opposite sex.
   ○ My parents' anger.
   ○ Other _____.

2. In the midst of your childhood fears, who was your biggest encourager?

   ○ A parent.
   ○ A sibling.
   ○ A grandparent.
   ○ A teacher.
   ○ A friend.
   ○ Other _____.

3. How has someone in this group been an encouragement to you?

Bible Study Read Scripture and Discuss (30 minutes)

After thanking God for the Philippians and sharing with them how he was doing in prison, Paul goes on to discuss how they should be living their lives as Christians. He did this not as an interfering busybody, but as a teacher who was concerned for his pupils. The Philippians were still young in the faith, and many of them came out of a Greek culture that was less stringent in terms of behavioral codes and expectations. He wanted to make sure that how they lived was a good witness to Jesus Christ. Read Philippians 1:27–2:4 and note how Paul talks about the importance of attitude and actions.

Leader

Select two members of the group ahead of time to read aloud the Scripture passage. Then discuss the Questions for Interaction, dividing into subgroups of three to six.

Right Living

Reader One: ²⁷Just one thing: live your life in a manner worthy of the gospel of Christ. Then, whether I come and see you or am absent, I will hear about you that you are standing firm in one spirit,

Reader Two: with one mind,

Reader One: working side by side for the faith of the gospel, ²⁸not being frightened in any way by your opponents. This is evidence of their destruction, but of your deliverance—and this is from God. ²⁹For it has been given to you on Christ's behalf not only to believe in Him,

Reader Two: but also to suffer for Him,

Reader One: ³⁰having the same struggle that you saw I had and now hear about me.

Reader Two: 2 If then there is any encouragement in Christ,

Reader One: if any consolation of love,

Reader Two: if any fellowship with the Spirit,

Reader One: if any affection and mercy,

Reader Two: [2]fulfill my joy by thinking the same way, having the same love, sharing the same feelings, focusing on one goal. [3]Do nothing out of rivalry or conceit, but in humility consider others as more important than yourselves. [4]Everyone should look out not only for his own interests, but also for the interests of others.

Philippians 1:27–2:4

Questions for Interaction

Leader
Refer to the Summary and Study Notes at the end of this section as needed. If 30 minutes is not enough time to answer all of the questions in this section, conclude the Bible Study by answering question 7.

1. How do you generally feel when someone tries to instruct you on how to live your life?

   ○ Defensive.
   ○ Cared for.
   ○ Rebellious.
   ○ Willing to learn.
   ○ It depends on who it is.
   ○ Other _____.

2. If you had known nothing of Paul previous to reading this passage, what impression would you get from what you read here?

   ○ He's a little too controlling for me.
   ○ He's kind of paternalistic.
   ○ He's "Mister Positive"!
   ○ He's very self-giving.
   ○ Other _____.

3. What does Paul mean by living "life in a manner worthy of the gospel of Christ"? What does the rest of this passage say that helps define this phrase?

4. Does what Paul says here mean that we have to agree on every issue (see notes on 2:2)? What kind of unity is important above all?

5. What are two things that will destroy Christian community (2:3)? How have you seen this at work yourself?

6. What are two things that will keep a Christian community from such problems (2:3–4)?

7. How well are you doing right now balancing your own interests with the interests of others? What examples can you point to as times where you put the interests of others over your self-interest? What do you need to start doing to have a better balance?

8. How well is your church doing at sharing the same feelings and focusing on one goal (2:2)? What can members of your group do to bring a greater sense of unity to your church?

Caring Time Apply the Lesson and Pray for One Another (15 minutes)

Comfort and encourage one another with this time of sharing and prayer. Begin by sharing your responses to the following questions. Be sure to offer any prayer requests and concerns before closing in prayer.

Leader
Begin the Caring Time by having group members take turns sharing responses to all three questions. Be sure to save at least the last five minutes for a time of prayer. Ask two volunteers to pray, remembering to pray for the empty chair.

1. What fear is most likely to keep you from being a bold witness for Jesus?

2. Pray for the unity of the church, not only your local congregation, but the church as a whole.

3. What are some "interests of others" that you need to take to God in prayer? What are some of your own interests that need similar prayer attention?

NEXT WEEK *Today we looked at what Paul had to say about living a life worthy of the Gospel, including having a spirit of attention to the interests of others. In the coming week, ask the Holy Spirit to help you focus on the one goal of living your life for Jesus. Next week we will consider how Christ gave us the greatest example of humility when he gave up equality with God and came to be part of this earthly life.*

Summary: Paul now shifts his focus from himself (a report on his situation) to the Philippians (advice on how to conduct themselves during difficult times). The pronouns shift from "I" (in 1:12–26) to "you" in this new section (1:27–2:4). Paul began this letter by writing about his difficulties and in so doing, allowed the Philippians to see how he dealt with pressure. Now he turns to their problems and offers insights that will enable them to cope with the opposition they face. Paul first exhorts the Philippians to be unified and without fear (1:27–30). Then he tells them that unity is achieved by means of self-sacrificing humility (2:1–4).

1:27 *live your life.* Literally, "be a good citizen." The Greek concept of citizenship involved the idea of cooperation, interdependence and mutuality, out of which each citizen attained his or her highest potential while assisting other to do the same. *standing firm.* This is a military term that conjures up images of a phalanx of Roman soldiers standing back to back, protecting each other while resisting the enemy. As long as everyone remained standing in his place, such a formation was virtually impenetrable.

1:28 *not being frightened.* Yet another rare word used in the Bible only this one time. Its original reference was to horses that were timid and shied easily. The Philippians must not let their opponents spook them into an uncontrolled stampede. *your opponents.* Paul does not identify their opponents. Nevertheless, in verse 30 he says, "having the same struggle that you saw I had and now hear about me." In both instances, Paul's opposition came from people who were opposed to his life and behavior as a Christian. In Philippi, this opposition came from secular merchants who were angry that he had freed a slave girl from bondage to an evil spirit.

1:29 *it has been given to you.* It is assumed that Christians will suffer. However, this is not something one has to put up with reluctantly (add a comma) because suffering for the sake of Christ is a gift of grace. Suffering is a privilege that has been granted to the Philippians. *on*

Christ's behalf. There are three senses in which this phrase can be interpreted. First, it could mean that they suffer "for Christ," i.e., because they are on his side, his enemies will harass them. Second, it could mean that they suffer "for the sake of Christ," i.e., because they love Christ they are willing to endure such difficulties. Or, third, it can mean (as it is correctly rendered in the HCSB) that they suffer "on Christ's behalf". Their aim is to "complete what is lacking in Christ's afflictions for the sake of his body, that is, the church," as Paul says in Colossians 1:24(RSV).

1:30 *the same struggle.* Paul alludes to two incidents of persecution known by the Philippians: the one in Philippi on his first visit there (Acts 16:16–40) and the other in Jerusalem that resulted in his present imprisonment (Acts 21:27–26:32). In each instance, Paul's struggle was with those who were opposed to his Christian beliefs and practices. In both cases, his opponents stirred up the crowds against him and forc.d the Roman authorities to take him into custody. It is important to note that Paul was not being persecuted by Rome. His persecution originated with opponents of the Gospel. The Philippians are also facing the same sort of opponents.

2:1 By means of four clauses, Paul urges the Philippians to say "Yes" to his request that they live together in harmony. They have a strong incentive to be united to one another because of their experience of the encouragement, love, fellowship, mercy and compassion of God the Father, Son and Holy Spirit. *If.* In Greek, this construction assumes a positive response, e.g., "If then there is any encouragement in Christ, which of course there is ... "

2:2 *thinking the same way.* Paul is not just urging everyone to hold identical ideas and opinions. The word for "think" is far more comprehensive and involves one's mind, but also one's feelings, attitudes and will. Paul is calling for a far deeper form of unity than simple doctrinal conformity. *sharing the same feelings.* In Greek, this is a single word that Paul probably made up since it is found nowhere else.

2:3 *rivalry.* This the second time Paul has used this word (see note on 1:17 in Session 2). It means working to advance oneself without thought for others. *conceit.* This is the only occurrence of this word in the New Testament. Translated literally, it means "vain glory" (*kenodoxia*) which is asserting oneself over God who alone is worthy of true glory (*doxa*). This is the sort of person who will arrogantly assert that he or she is right even though what that person holds is false. This is a person whose concern is for personal prestige. *humility.* This was not a virtue that was valued by the Greek in the first century. They considered this to be the attitude of a slave. In the Old Testament, however, this was understood to be the proper attitude to hold before God. Christians are to accord others the same dignity and respect that Christ has given to all people. Humility involves seeing others not on the basis of how clever, attractive or pious they are, but through the eyes of Christ (who died for them).

2:4 *for his own interests.* Preoccupation with personal interests, along with selfish ambition and vain conceit, make unity impossible. Individualism or partisanship work against community. Note that Paul says, "Everyone should look out not only for his own interests." Personal interests are important, but not to the exclusion of everything else.

Imitating Christ

Scripture Philippians 2:5–11

LAST WEEK *In last week's session, we saw what Paul had to say about how the Christian should live. We were reminded of the importance of unity among Christians and how we need to demonstrate love and humility, considering others to be more important than ourselves. This week we will focus on Christ's incredible example of humility, as he gave up the glory of heaven and came down to earth to become the sacrifice for our salvation.*

 Ice-Breaker Connect with Your Group (15 minutes)

Leader
Begin the session with a word of prayer. Choose one, two or all three of the Ice-Breaker questions. Welcome and introduce new group members.

There's an old country song that says, "Oh Lord, it's hard to be humble when you're perfect in every way!" Jesus was perfect as he lived on this earth, but he would never have sung that song. He is certainly the best role model we could ever look to for the virtue of humility. Take turns sharing your experiences and thoughts about having role models and being humble.

1. Growing up, who was your role? Why did you admire that person?

2. Which of the following would take the most humility for you to do?

   ○ Cleaning the bathroom toilets.
   ○ Admitting to a family member I was wrong.
   ○ Riding public transportation to school or work.
   ○ Socializing with people of a lower station.
   ○ Taking care of a bedridden person.
   ○ Other _____.

3. If you were to rank yourself today on a "humble-meter" from 1 ("I am only worthy to be here by God's grace") to 10 ("My exemplary humility is only one of my many excellent qualities"), what level would you choose?

Bible Study Read Scripture and Discuss (30 minutes)

Leader
Select two members of the group ahead of time to read aloud the Scripture passage. Then discuss the Questions for Interaction, dividing into subgroups of three to six.

After mentioning the need for humility in the previous verses (2:3–4), Paul now goes on to point to Christ as the model for living a humble life. Jesus especially showed this humility by being willing to give up his status of unity with God the Father in heaven to take on human form and experience human suffering here on earth. If Christ were willing to do that, shouldn't we be willing to do humble acts to serve him as well? Read Philippians 2:5–11 and note all that Jesus gave up to save us.

Imitating Christ

Reader One: [5]Make your own attitude that of Christ Jesus,

> [6]who, existing in the form of God,
> did not consider equality with God
> as something to be used for His own advantage.

Reader Two: [7]Instead He emptied Himself
> by assuming the form of a slave,
> taking on the likeness of men.
> And when He had come as a man in His external form,

Reader One: [8]He humbled Himself
> by becoming obedient to the point of death—
> even to death on a cross.
> [9]For this reason God also highly exalted Him
> and gave Him the name
> that is above every name,

Reader Two: [10]so that at the name of Jesus
> every knee should bow—
> of those who are in heaven
> and on earth and under the earth—
> [11]and every tongue should confess
> that Jesus Christ is Lord,
> to the glory of God the Father.

Philippians 2:5–11

Questions for Interaction

Leader
Refer to the Summary and Study Notes at the end of this section as needed. If 30 minutes is not enough time to answer all of the questions in this section, conclude the Bible Study by answering questions 6 and 7.

1. Which phrase best expresses how you feel about the idea your attitude should be "that of Christ Jesus"?

   ○ "Oh, sure!—that's going to happen!"
   ○ "That may work for Billy Graham or Mother Teresa, but it's not me."
   ○ "Sure—reach for the moon!"
   ○ "I'll get by with a little help from my friends—and God!"
   ○ "What God calls us to do, God strengthens us to do."
   ○ Other _____.

2. What would you say is the most amazing thing that is mentioned in this passage?

   ○ That one who was God could also be humble.
   ○ That Christ loved us enough to choose to go through suffering for us.
   ○ That one day "every knee" will bow to Christ.
   ○ Other _____.

3. Verse 5 says, "Make your own attitude that of Christ Jesus." What is his attitude? From what it says here and what else you know of him in Scripture, how did he manifest this attitude?

4. Why did Christ give up his position and power as the Son of God (vv. 6–7)?

5. How does this passage challenge society's definition of success? What is your definition of success?

6. Christ was obedient even to death on the cross. At what point do you find yourself most challenged when it comes to being obedient to God?

   ○ When it comes to endangering my physical safety.
   ○ When it comes to endangering the physical safety of my loved ones.
   ○ When it comes to risking rejection by my friends.
   ○ When it comes to trying something challenging where I might fail.
   ○ When it comes to giving up an addictive behavior.
   ○ Other _____.

7. What is one specific way you can imitate Christ's humility this coming week?

8. This ancient hymn speaks of "every knee bowing" and "every tongue confessing" Christ. Does this mean that at some point all will come to Christ, or simply that at some point even nonbelievers will realize they were wrong (see notes on verses 10–11)?

Caring Time Apply the Lesson and Pray for One Another **(15 minutes)**

Take some time now to support one another in prayer and to thank Jesus for all he has done for you. Before closing in prayer, take turns sharing your answers to the following questions.

Leader
Be sure to save at least 15 minutes for this important time. After sharing responses to all three questions and asking for prayer requests, close in a time of group prayer.

1. What season are you experiencing in your spiritual life right now?

   ○ The warmth of summer.
   ○ The dead of winter.
   ○ The new life of spring.
   ○ The changes of fall.

2. How would you like to thank Jesus for what he did for you by coming to this world to suffer?

3. In what ways are you going through suffering right now? How can this group be supportive?

NEXT WEEK *Today we looked at how Christ demonstrated humility by choosing to be part of the suffering of this earthly life. We were reminded of all that he gave up to provide a way for our salvation. In the coming week, take some time to appreciate God's majesty in nature (perhaps watch the stars come out) and thank him for his goodness and love. Next week we will consider some of the pastoral concerns Paul had for the Philippian church, and what they might say to us today.*

Summary: From a theological point of view, this is the most important section of Philippians. Here Paul provides an amazing glimpse into the nature of Jesus Christ. Through Paul's eyes we see Jesus, the divine Savior, who comes to his people in humility and not in power; we see the Lord of the Universe before whom all bow, choosing to die for his subjects; we see one who is in nature God, voluntarily descending to the depths before he is lifted up to the heights. This is a breathtaking glimpse that is made all the more astonishing because no one ever imagined that God would work his will in such a way. Who would have thought that God would act through weakness and not through power?

It is to demonstrate the humility of Christ that Paul quotes from an ancient Christian hymn about Jesus. In quoting this hymn, Paul provides a fascinating glimpse into how the early Christians viewed Jesus. He also gives us one of the few existing examples of early church hymnology.

2:5 This is a transitional verse in which Paul states that the model for the sort of self-sacrificing humility he has been urging is found in Jesus.

2:6–11 There is little agreement between scholars as to how this hymn breaks into verses or how it is to be phrased. However, one thing is clear. The hymn has two equal parts. Part one (vv. 6–8) focuses on the self-humiliation of Jesus. Part two (vv. 9–11) focuses on God's exaltation of Jesus. In part one, Jesus is the subject of the two main verbs; while in part two, God is the subject of the two main verbs.

2:6 the form of God. The Greek word here is *morphe* (used twice by Paul in this hymn). He says that Jesus was in his nature (form) God, but that he then took upon himself the form or nature of a slave (v. 7). This is a key word in understanding the nature of Christ. Jesus possessed the essential nature of God. *to be used for His advantage.* This translates a rare word, used only at this point in the New Testament. The Holman Christian Standard Bible points out that while Jesus was God, he did not look upon that as something to exempt him from the possibility of human suffering.

2:7 emptied Himself. Literally, "to pour out until the container is empty." This could be interpreted to mean that Christ stripped himself of all of the "rights and privileges" that would normally come with his status, so that he might face life with the same disadvantages as the rest of us human beings. *assuming the form of a slave.* Jesus gave up Godhood and took on slavehood. From being the ultimate master, he became the lowest slave. He left ruling for serving. *Morphe* is used here again, indicating that Jesus adopted the essential nature of a slave. *taking on the likeness of men.* The point is not that Jesus just seemed to be human. He assumed the identity of a person and was similar in all ways to other human beings. *as a man in His external form.* The word translated "external form" is *schema*, and denotes that which is outward and changeable (in contrast to) *morphe*, which denotes that which is essential and eternal). In other words, Jesus was a true man, but only temporarily.

2:8 He humbled Himself. This is the central point that Paul wants to make. This is why he offered this illustration. Jesus is the ultimate model of one who lived a life of self-sacrifice, self-renunciation and self-surrender. Jesus existed at the pinnacle and yet descended to the very base. There has never been a more radical humbling. Furthermore, this was not something forced upon Jesus, he voluntarily chose this. *obedient to the point of death.* The extent of this humbling is defined by this clause. Jesus humbled himself to the furthest point one could go. He submitted to death itself for the sake of both God and humanity. There was no more dramatic way to demonstrate humility. *death on a cross.* This was no ordinary death. For one thing, it came about in an unusually cruel way. Crucifixion was a harsh, demeaning and utterly painful way to die. For another thing, according to the Old Testament, those who died by hanging on a tree were considered cursed by God. For a Jew there was no more humiliating way to die. Jesus, who was equal to God, died like an accused criminal. His descent from glory had brought him as low as one could go.

2:9 The self-humiliation of Jesus is followed by the God-induced exaltation of Jesus. Jesus descended to the depths and was raised again to the heights. *name.* In the ancient world, a name was more than just a way of distinguishing one individual from another. It revealed the inner nature or character of a person. The name given the resurrected Jesus is the supreme name—the name above all names—because this is who Jesus is in his innermost being.

2:10 *Jesus.* It is significant that the one before whom all will bow is Jesus, the man from Nazareth. The cosmic Lord is none other than the person who walked the roads of Palestine and talked to the people of Israel. He had a hometown, a family, a trade and disciples. The one before whom Christians will stand at the Last Judgment is not an anonymous Life Force, but the man of Galilee who has a familiar face.

2:11 *Jesus Christ is Lord.* This is the earliest and most basic confession of faith on the part of the church (Acts 2:36; Rom. 10:9; 1 Cor. 12:3). *Lord.* This is the name that was given to Jesus, the name that reflects who he really is (v. 9). This is the name of God. Jesus is the supreme Sovereign of the universe.

Shining Like Stars

Scripture Philippians 2:12–30

> **LAST WEEK** *"He humbled himself by becoming obedient to the point of death" (2:8). Last week we considered how imitating Christ's humility is an essential part of living the Christian life. We were reminded of how much we have to thank God for in sending his Son to die for us. This week we will look at how Paul showed his pastoral concern for the Philippians, and how following his leadership would make them "shine like stars."*

Ice-Breaker Connect With Your Group (15 minutes)

There are many things every day that can cause us to be fearful or grumpy and argumentative. How about the last time someone cut you off in traffic? Take turns sharing some of your experiences with these emotions.

1. When you were in grade school, what was most likely to cause you "fear and trembling"?

   ○ The angry voice of my father or mother.
   ○ Watching late-night horror movies.
   ○ Thunderstorms.
   ○ The neighborhood bully.
   ○ Having to face my teacher with homework that wasn't finished.
   ○ A "haunted" house in the neighborhood.
   ○ Other _____.

Leader
Begin the session with a word of prayer. If there are new group members, remember to welcome and introduce them. Also, do all three Ice-Breaker questions to help them get acquainted.

2. What were you most likely to grumble and argue about when you were in grade school?

　　○ Household chores.
　　○ What there was to eat.
　　○ Having to go to church.
　　○ Having to do homework instead of playing or watching TV.
　　○ Having to watch out after a younger sibling.
　　○ Other _____.

3. What are you most likely to grumble about today?

 Bible Study Read Scripture and Discuss (30 minutes)

In this passage, Paul first admonishes the Philippians toward "stellar" behavior and then goes on to share his plans concerning how he was going to keep in touch with them and their needs. This is a good example of how Paul had a constant concern for those who were his spiritual children. Read Philippians 2:12–30 and note the important witness that Christian behavior is to the rest of the world.

Leader
Select a member of the group ahead of time to read aloud the Scripture passage. Then discuss the Questions for Interaction, dividing into subgroups of three to six.

Shining Like Stars

[12]So then, my dear friends, just as you have always obeyed, not only in my presence, but now even more in my absence, work out your own salvation with fear and trembling. [13]For it is God who is working in you, enabling you both to will and to act for His good purpose. [14]Do everything without grumbling and arguing, [15]so that you may be blameless and pure, children of God who are faultless in a crooked and perverted generation, among whom you shine like stars in the world. [16]Hold firmly the message of life. Then I can boast in the day of Christ that I didn't run in vain or labor for nothing. [17]But even if I am poured out as a drink offering on the sacrifice and service of your faith, I am glad and rejoice with all of you. [18]In the same way you also should rejoice and share your joy with me.

[19]Now I hope in the Lord Jesus to send Timothy to you soon so that I also may be encouraged when I hear news about you. [20]For I have no one else like-minded who will genuinely care about your interests; [21]all seek their own interests, not those of Jesus Christ. [22]But you know his proven character, because he has served with me in the gospel ministry like a son with a father. [23]Therefore, I hope to send him as soon as I see how things go with me. [24]And I am convinced in the Lord that I myself will also come quickly.

[25]But I considered it necessary to send you Epaphroditus—my brother, co-worker, and fellow soldier, as well as your messenger and minister to my need— [26]since he has been longing for all of you and was distressed because you heard that he was sick. [27]Indeed, he was so sick that he nearly died. However, God had mercy on him, and not only on him but also on me, so that I would not have one

grief on top of another. [28]For this reason, I am very eager to send him so that you may rejoice when you see him again and I may be less anxious. [29]Therefore, welcome him in the Lord with all joy and hold men like him in honor, [30]because he came close to death for the work of Christ, risking his life to make up what was lacking in your ministry to me.

Philippians 2:12–30

Questions for Interaction

Leader
Refer to the Summary and Study Notes at the end of this section as needed. If 30 minutes is not enough time to answer all of the questions in this section, conclude the Bible Study by answering question 7.

1. Who does Paul sound like in this passage?

   ○ My boss.
   ○ An army sergeant.
   ○ A coach at halftime.
   ○ A parent writing to a child who is away.
   ○ A preacher.
   ○ A concerned friend.
   ○ Other _____.

2. If a "Paul" were to look for someone to send to you, to look out after your welfare, which of the following qualities would it be most important to you that this emissary have?

   ○ Humility.
   ○ The ability to listen.
   ○ Being nonjudgmental.
   ○ Having a sense of humor.
   ○ Showing real understanding.
   ○ Other _____.

3. What does it mean to "work out your own salvation" (see note on v. 12)? What is the relationship between salvation and our works?

4. What is God's responsibility and what is ours for achieving God's "good purpose" (vv. 12–13; see notes on v. 13)?

5. What are some of Timothy's qualities that caused Paul to decide to send him to the Philippians (vv. 19–24)? How do these qualities compare to what you discussed in question 2?

6. What is the closest you have come to having a "spiritual parent" (v. 22)? What is the closest you have come to having a "spiritual child"?

7. On a scale of 1 (dim flashlight) to 10 (bright star), how brightly do you "shine" in your "universe"? What one personal change would help you to shine a little brighter?

Going Deeper If your group has time and/or wants a challenge, go on to this question.

8. What does Paul mean when he speaks of the possibility of his being "poured out as a drink offering" (v. 17)? What kind of qualities does a person need to have to be willing to suffer and sacrifice for someone else's faith?

 Caring Time Apply the Lesson and Pray for One Another (15 minutes)

Come together now for this time of sharing and prayer, remembering that "it is God who is working in you, enabling you both to will and to act for His good purpose" (v. 13).

1. How did you see God working in your life this past week?

2. How can this group show the qualities to each other that we talked about in questions 2 and 5 of the ions for Interaction? Pray that this group can show such qualities to each other.

3. Take time to thank God for the "Timothys" who have been sent to you in your lifetime.

Leader
Encourage everyone to participate in this important time and be sure that each group member is receiving prayer support. Continue to pray for the empty chair in the closing group prayer.

NEXT WEEK *Today we considered how important it is to "shine as stars" in our world and demonstrate the love of God through our actions and attitudes. In the coming week, show some extra kindness to people. Even a smile can brighten someone's day. Next week we will focus on what it means to put everything else aside in order to reach the goal of becoming more and more like Christ.*

Summary: Paul ends this section with an exhortation to the Philippians that they obey him by doing what he has been urging them to do—namely, they must forsake selfishness, conceit, pride, grumbling and argument. These are the attitudes that have led to the disunity that now threatens their whole community. Instead they must work at bringing health ("salvation") to their church.

Although this is a new section and Paul has shifted his focus away from the problem of disunity in the Philippian church, what he says here is connected to the previous section. When discussing the kind of lifestyle that led to unity, Paul offered two examples of self-giving sacrifice. First, there was the unparalleled example of Jesus Christ, who, though he was God, became a servant of humankind. Second, Paul offered his own willingness to be "poured out as a drink offering" as another example of how they ought to be living

2:12 *my dear friends.* This is a single Greek word that means literally, "beloved." *obeyed.* Paul links the hymn about Jesus to the experience of the Philippians through the word "obey." In the same way that Christ was obedient even to death (2:8), so too they should obey his apostolic injunctions. Such obedience ought not to be distasteful to the Philippians since they have "always obeyed." The word "obey" carries with it the idea of "hearing" and then "submitting" to what is heard. *work out your own salvation.* To understand what Paul is urging on them, it is important to understand how the word "salvation" is used here. The Greek word translated "salvation" has several meanings in the New Testament. It can refer to the saving work of God in the life of a Christian that begins here and now, and is completed in the Day of Judgment. This word can also mean "health and wholeness." The context of this verse indicates that Paul is thinking of the whole community and not the individual Christian. Furthermore, the word "your" is plural. This is the broader sense of the Greek word that is probably intended. *fear and trembling.* This phrase can refer to the awe that a creature feels when standing before the Creator, and which drives him or her to seek and to do the will of God. It can also refer to an attitude of obedience toward God.

2:13 *it is God who is working in you.* The word for "works" is *energein,* from which the English word "energy" is derived. By this phrase Paul seeks to indicate that the power of God is already at work within the Philippian church. In order for spiritual harmony to come, they must therefore avail themselves of this power. *to will and to act.* God promotes both the desire to do his will and the drive necessary to accomplish it.

2:14 *grumbling.* This is the same sort of mumbling and grumbling against the leaders of the community that characterized Israel in the wilderness (Ex. 15:24). *arguing.* This is useless and ill-tempered. Both grumbling and arguing create divisions within a community.

2:15 *blameless/pure/faultless.* A description of what the Philippians should strive to become. In relationship to the outside world, they are to be blameless; i.e., the kind of people against whom no accusation can be laid. In relationship to themselves, they are to be as pure as metal that is unmixed with an alloy. In relationship to God, they are to be as faultless as an unblemished sacrificial animal.

2:16 *message of life.* The Gospel that Paul and the Philippians preached. *day of Christ.* The Day of Judgment, when all people will stand before Christ. Since Christians will be called upon to give account of how well they used the gifts entrusted to them (1 Cor. 4:1–5), Paul urges the Philippians to continue to obey the demands of the Gospel. *run ... or labor.* Paul describes his ministry by means of two metaphors. The image of "running" comes from the world of sports, and pictures an athlete straining to reach the finish line (3:12–14; Gal. 2:2). The second image comes from the world of work, and describes labor to the point of exhaustion.

2:17 Paul hastens to point out the fact of their own "sacrifice and service," lest they feel that he is too critical of them (or that he has no confidence in them). Their past acts of love and service demonstrate their commitment. *poured out as a drink offering.* His specific reference is to the practice of pouring out a libation (a glass of wine or olive oil) over the altar as a part of the sacrificial ritual. He may be admitting here the possibility that he might *not* survive this imprisonment as he expressed hope that he would (1:23–26). In that case his death would be like a sacrifice poured out for the benefit of the Philippians, as well as his other children in the faith (note he says "even if ... " this might occur). It is possible, however, that the "sacrifice" he refers to is simply his suffering in prison.

2:19 *in the Lord Jesus.* Paul is not making these plans solely on the basis of his own will and desire. He is seeking to follow God's leading in this matter. This is a good example of the principle he just enunciated, whereby Christians are to live in the tension between actively working out their own salvation while simultaneously depending upon God to work his will in their lives (2:12–13). *Timothy.* This is Paul's long-time friend and coworker who was with him when he founded the church in Philippi. This is not the first time that Paul has sent Timothy on

a mission. Previously, he sent Timothy to Thessalonica from Athens (1 Thess. 3:1–10) and to Corinth from Ephesus (1 Cor. 4:17; 16:10–11). *that I also may be encouraged when I hear news about you.* Paul has two reasons for sending Timothy. First, he knows that the news Timothy will bring back to him about their situation will encourage him greatly while he is confined in prison. Second, by implication, Paul wants the Philippians to be cheered up when Timothy gives them the news of Paul's situation. (Paul says, "that I also may be encouraged" implying that the Philippians had already been cheered up.)

2:20 *like-minded.* This is a rare Greek word that means "one who shares the same feelings." By using the word, Paul conveys the fact that Timothy comes in his name and speaks on his behalf. In other words, in hearing Timothy, they are hearing Paul.

2:22 *his proven character.* The Greek word used here indicates that Timothy has been tested in difficult situations and has come through them successfully.

2:25 *Epaphroditus.* Epaphroditus had been sent by the Philippian church to convey a gift to Paul, and then to stay on as a member of Paul's apostolic group. However, he fell ill. The church heard about this and became quite anxious about him. In addition, Epaphroditus was homesick. For both reasons, Paul senses that it is time for Epaphroditus to return to Philippi.

2:27 Paul confirms that the rumor they heard was true: Epaphroditus had been close to death. Paul goes on to say that his recovery was due to God. *one grief on top of another.* The recovery of Epaphroditus spared Paul from literally "wave upon wave" of grief. Although his own death might seem at times a great gain for him

(1:21–23), Paul was not immune to the sorrow that comes when friends die.

2:30 *risking his life.* A gambling term, it denotes one who risked everything on the roll of the dice. In the post-apostolic church, some Christians took Epaphroditus as their model. They called themselves "The Gamblers," and deliberately risked their lives for the sake of the Gospel. They visited prisons, cared for the sick (even those with contagious diseases), buried victims of the plague, etc.

Pressing on Toward Christ

Scripture Philippians 3:1–21

LAST WEEK *In last week's session, we looked at how Paul encouraged the Philippians to "shine like stars" in a "crooked and perverted generation" (2:15). We also saw him show his pastoral concern for the Philippians by sending them Timothy as a pastor and teacher. Today we will see what Paul says about not "resting on our laurels," but pressing on to be like Christ.*

 Ice-Breaker Connect With Your Group (15 minutes)

It's always a great feeling to achieve a goal or receive an honor. Paul considered the greatest goal in his life to be "the prize promised by God's heavenly call in Christ Jesus" (v. 14). Take turns sharing your experiences with goals and honors.

Leader
Begin the session with a word of prayer, asking God for his blessing and presence. Choose one, two or all three of the Ice-Breaker questions, depending on your group's needs.

1. Which of the following prizes or honors do you wish you could have won in high school?

   ○ Most Likely to Succeed.
   ○ Homecoming King or Queen.
   ○ Most Valuable Player.
   ○ Class President.
   ○ Valedictorian.
   ○ Other _____.

2. What prize or honor are you most proud of receiving as an adult?

3. What possession do you have that you would give up everything else to retain? What makes this so valuable to you?

Bible Study Read Scripture and Discuss (30 minutes)

Leader
Ask two members of the group, selected ahead of time, to read aloud the Scripture passage. Have one person read verses 1–11; and the other read verses 12–21. Then discuss the Questions for Interaction, dividing into subgroups of three to six.

Having written about his past and present, as well as his relationship to the Philippians, Paul now looks at where he is going. He was not one to "stand pat" or rest on what he had already accomplished. He was always looking to do more. For him that meant setting everything else aside, so that he might reach his goal of being like Christ. That is the spirit Paul had and the spirit he sought to engender in others. Read Philippians 3:1–21 and note the results of focusing on earthly things, rather than spiritual things.

Pressing on Toward Christ

Reader One: 3 Finally, my brothers, rejoice in the Lord. To write to you again about this is no trouble for me and is a protection for you. ²Watch out for "dogs," watch out for evil workers, watch out for those who mutilate the flesh. ³For we are the circumcision, the ones who serve by the Spirit of God, boast in Christ Jesus, and do not put confidence in the flesh— ⁴although I once had confidence in the flesh too. If anyone else thinks he has grounds for confidence in the flesh, I have more: ⁵circumcised the eighth day; of the nation of Israel, of the tribe of Benjamin, a Hebrew born of Hebrews; as to the law, a Pharisee; ⁶as to zeal, persecuting the church; as to the righteousness that is in the law, blameless. ⁷But everything that was a gain to me, I have considered to be a loss because of Christ. ⁸More than that, I also consider everything to be a loss in view of the surpassing value of knowing Christ Jesus my Lord. Because of Him I have suffered the loss of all things and consider them filth, so that I may gain Christ ⁹and be found in Him, not having a righteousness of my own from the law, but one that is through faith in Christ—the righteousness from God based on faith. ¹⁰My goal is to know Him and the power of His resurrection and the fellowship of His sufferings, being conformed to His death, ¹¹assuming that I will somehow reach the resurrection from among the dead.

Reader Two: ¹²Not that I have already reached the goal or am already fully mature, but I make every effort to take hold of it because I also have been taken hold of by Christ Jesus. ¹³Brothers, I do not consider myself to have taken hold of it. But one thing I do: forgetting what is behind and reaching forward to what is ahead, ¹⁴I pursue as my goal the prize promised by God's heavenly call in Christ Jesus. ¹⁵Therefore, all who are mature should think this way. And if you think differently about anything, God will reveal this to you also. ¹⁶In any case, we should live up to whatever truth we have attained. ¹⁷Join in imitating me, brothers, and observe those who live according to the example you have in us. ¹⁸For I have often told you, and now say again with tears, that many live as enemies of the cross of Christ. ¹⁹Their end is destruction; their god is their stomach;

their glory is in their shame. They are focused on earthly things, [20]but our citizenship is in heaven, from which we also eagerly wait for a Savior, the Lord Jesus Christ. [21]He will transform the body of our humble condition into the likeness of His glorious body, by the power that enables Him to subject everything to Himself.

Philippians 3:1–21

Questions for Interaction

Leader
Refer to the Summary and Study Notes at the end of this section as needed. If 30 minutes is not enough time to answer all of the questions in this section, conclude the Bible Study by answering questions 6 and 7.

1. What or who are the "dogs" in your life you have to watch out for?

2. What would you say are your grounds for confidence in yourself?

   ○ The talents God has given me.
   ○ My history of success.
   ○ My good looks.
   ○ My experience that God has always been with me.
   ○ What confidence in myself?
   ○ Other _____.

3. What were the traits or experiences that Paul put his confidence in prior to his conversion (vv. 4–6)? Why might he have put confidence in such things?

4. In his "profit and loss" accounting system (vv. 4–8), how does Paul ultimately figure the worth of his religious credentials?

5. What was Paul trying to forget, and what was he trying to keep his life focused on? What was the ultimate goal of such efforts, and why was forgetting the past important to such efforts?

6. If you compared your spiritual life right now to a track race (as Paul was doing in vv. 12–14), where would you be in the race right now?

7. Of the directions in this chapter, which do you need to take to heart in order to run a better race?

   ○ Get the "dogs" to stop harassing me (v. 2).
   ○ Stop putting my confidence in my worldly status (vv. 4–5).
   ○ Get my priorities straight and count lesser things as "loss" (v. 7).
   ○ Be willing to suffer a little (v. 10).
   ○ Forget my past mistakes (v. 13).
   ○ Forget my past successes (v. 13).
   ○ Focus only on the goal of Christ (v. 14).

8. What is the role of suffering in "winning the race" as well as in being part of the fellowship of Christ?

 Caring Time Apply the Lesson and Pray for One Another (15 minutes)

Spending time in prayer is one of the key components to achieving the goal of spiritual maturity and being more and more like Christ. Help each other toward this goal now with a time of sharing and prayer.

1. Where are you struggling in your "race" right now? How can this group best be of support to you?

2. What can you do in the coming week to balance the time you spend on spiritual activities with all of your other responsibilities?

3. How do you need Christ to "transform" (v. 21) your life in the coming year?

Leader
Following the Caring Time, discuss with your group how they would like to celebrate the last session next week. Also, discuss the possibility of splitting into two groups and continuing with another study.

NEXT WEEK *Today we considered the race we run as Christians and what it means to put everything else aside in order to reach the goal of becoming more and more like Christ. In the coming week, do some planning on how you can spend more time on spiritual growth. Next week we will focus on the reasons that we can rejoice in all circumstances.*

Summary: Paul now turns his attention to the false teachers who are troubling the church at Philippi. First, he describes them by means of three rather vivid terms (dogs, evildoers, mutilators (v. 2). Then, he points out the error in their teaching. They are saying that it is by keeping the Law that one gains God's favor (v. 3). To demonstrate that righteousness is not attained in this way, Paul describes his own background (vv. 4–6). He was the most orthodox of Jews and yet when he met Jesus on the Damascus Road, he came to realize that all his accomplishments and all the privileges afforded him because of his heritage were mere rubbish in comparison to knowing Christ (vv. 7–11). Paul then goes on to describe in more detail what it means to strive to take hold of Christ. Here he also warns against anyone who might feel that they have already "arrived" spiritually and thus attained "perfection."

3:1 *Finally.* It appears that Paul is about to conclude his letter. But in verse 2 he suddenly goes off in a whole new direction and issues a strong warning about the false teachers in Philippi. *rejoice in the Lord.* Paul continues to emphasize rejoicing. Here for the first time he adds the words "in the Lord." *protection.* Joy is a protection against those negative attitudes that bring disunity. A person who is rejoicing cannot simultaneously be grumbling or promoting his or her own interests.

3:2 *dogs.* A derogatory term used by many Jews in the first century to describe Gentiles, given its force by the fact that Jews considered to be unclean. Paul's Judaizing critics are, in fact, the real "dogs" because of the way in which they are perverting the truth of God. *those who mutilate the flesh.* In Greek, this is a pun that is difficult to translate. Paul is saying that their circumcision is really mutilation. Not only is it of no value, but it actually goes against God's will.

3:3 *boast in Christ Jesus.* The legalists within Judaism prided themselves in the Law and their observance of it, while those in Christ boasted of Jesus who had brought them righteousness. *do not put confidence in the flesh.* Here the word "flesh" probably means, "unredeemed human nature." Christians do not rely upon

personal striving as the basis for their righteousness.

3:4 *confidence in the flesh.* This is what these particular Jews are promoting: righteousness based on heritage and accomplishment.

3:5 *eighth day.* It was on the eighth day after birth that a Jewish (as opposed to a proselyte) was circumcised. Paul was a true Jew right from the time of his birth. *the tribe of Benjamin.* The members of the tribe of Benjamin constituted an elite group within Israel. *a Pharisee.* A spiritually elite group in Israel who emphasized the Law.

3:6 *as to zeal, persecuting the church.* Paul had demonstrated his zeal for the Law by ferreting out Christians and bringing them to trial (Acts 22:4–5; 26:9–11). *blameless.* To the best of his ability, Paul tried to observe the whole Law.

3:7 *gain/loss.* Paul describes his change in outlook in terms of a balance sheet. What was once on the "profit" side of the ledger (when he was a Pharisee) has been shifted over to the "loss" side (now that he is a Christian.)

3:8 *in view of the surpassing value of knowing Christ Jesus.* Paul discovered that only one thing had ultimate value—knowing Christ. It should be noted that knowing Christ in this way is not intellectual, but experiential. *filth.* This is really quite a vulgar term, and refers to either "waste food bound for the garbage pit" or "human dung."

3:10 *know.* The knowledge about which Paul speaks is personal knowledge and not just intellectual knowledge. *the power of His resurrection.* Paul wants to experience personally the resurrected Christ in all his power (Eph. 1:18–21). *the fellowship of His sufferings.* There is a fellowship that happens when people suffer together for a cause. When we suffer together to establish God's work, we have a fellowship with Christ and with each other that those not involved cannot know.

3:12 *Not that.* Paul does not claim that he has reached any sort of perfection in his spiritual life, or has fully comprehended who Christ is. *fully mature.* This is the only time in his epistles that Paul uses this word. Paul indicates that he has not yet fully understood Jesus Christ. There is simply too much to know of Christ ever to grasp it all this side of heaven. *make every effort.* The Christian life is one of relentless striving to know Christ in his fullness. *to take hold of it.* This can refer to winning a prize, as for example, in a race. Or it can mean to understand or comprehend something. *I also have been taken hold of by Christ Jesus.* Paul refers here to his conversion experience on the Damascus Road.

3:13 *consider.* This word means, "to calculate precisely." Paul means that after looking carefully at his life and all he has experienced of Christ, he has come to the conclusion that he has a long way to go in his spiritual pilgrimage. *forgetting what is behind.* In order to press on to a successful conclusion of his spiritual pilgrimage, Paul must first cease looking at his past. Neither

guilt nor personal attainment will assist him in gaining Christ.

3:14 *the prize.* What Paul seems to have in mind is the moment at the end of the race, when the games master calls the winner forward to receive the victory palm or wreath.

3:17 *imitating me.* Paul is calling them to imitate is his striving to find his goodness in Christ Jesus, his willingness to give himself sacrificially for the sake of others, and his deep passion to see the Gospel advanced (1:12–26; 3:7–11).

3:18 *with tears.* These are tears of frustration on Paul's part, that his beloved fellow Jews continue to reject the Gospel. *enemies of the cross.* It was the fact of Jesus' death that so scandalized the Jews. They found it almost impossible to accept that God could will and work through a crucified Messiah.

3:19 *destruction.* Since they reject the Cross (which lies at the heart of the way of salvation), their destiny is to live outside the life offered by God in Christ. *their god is their stomach.* The Jewish establishment was obsessed with laws relating to what they could eat and drink, how and when to eat, ritual preparation for eating, etc.

3:20 *citizenship.* In contrast to the Jewish teachers whose focus is on "earthly things" (v. 19), the focus of Christians is on heaven (where their true home lies).

3:21 *the body of our humble condition.* In contrast to those who taught that perfection was possible here and now, Christians knew that it was only at the Second Coming, by the work of Christ, that their frail, weak and corrupt bodies would be transformed into a spiritual body akin to Christ's "glorious body."

A Call to Rejoice

Scripture Philippians 4:1–23

LAST WEEK *Paul reminded us in last week's session that our goal in this life should focus on knowing Christ and becoming more like him, rather than focusing so much on "earthly things" (3:19). We also discussed how we should not be "resting on our laurels" or worrying about the past, but pressing on to spiritual maturity. This week we will come to appreciate how we can rejoice in all circumstances through Christ.*

Ice-Breaker Connect With Your Group (15 minutes)

Unity, joy and contentment! These are blessings that only God can provide and Paul has emphasized them throughout his letter to the Philippians. Take turns sharing about times in your life when you may or may not have experienced these blessings.

Leader
Begin this final session with a word of prayer and thanksgiving for this time together. Be sure to affirm each group member for the blessings and contributions that he or she made to the group.

1. Growing up, who in your family were you most likely to disagree with?

2. Who is the peacemaker in your family now? How does he or she do it?

3. When you were a child or teenager, what relative or family friend always sent the best gifts at Christmas or for your birthday? What gifts do you especially remember?

Bible Study Read Scripture and Discuss (30 minutes)

Paul concludes his letter with truly uplifting words. After urging some people in the church to make up with each other, he goes on to call them all to rejoice in the Lord always. While part of his own reason for rejoicing is a gift of support they had sent for him, he divulges the true and deeper reason behind his joy—through Christ he has learned to find peace and contentment in all circumstances. That is the spirit Paul seeks to convey to the Philippians as well. Read Philippians 4:1–23 and note the reasons for Paul's joy.

A Call to Rejoice

4 So then, in this way, my dearly loved brothers, my joy and crown, stand firm in the Lord, dear friends. [2]I urge Euodia and I urge Syntyche to agree in the Lord. [3]Yes, I also ask you, true partner, to help these women who have contended for the gospel at my side, along with Clement and the rest of my co-workers whose names are in the book of life. [4]Rejoice in the Lord always. I will say it again: Rejoice! [5]Let your graciousness be known to everyone. The Lord is near. [6]Don't worry about anything, but in everything, through prayer and petition with thanksgiving, let your requests be made known to God. [7]And the peace of God, which surpasses every thought, will guard your hearts and your minds in Christ Jesus.

[8]Finally brothers, whatever is true, whatever is honorable, whatever is just, whatever is pure, whatever is lovely, whatever is commendable—if there is any moral excellence and if there is any praise—dwell on these things. [9]Do what you have learned and received and heard and seen in me, and the God of peace will be with you.

[10]I rejoiced in the Lord greatly that now at last you have renewed your care for me. You were, in fact, concerned about me, but lacked the opportunity to show it. [11]I don't say this out of need, for I have learned to be content in whatever circumstances I am. [12]I know both how to have a little, and I know how to have a lot. In any and all circumstances I have learned the secret of being content—whether well-fed or hungry, whether in abundance or in need. [13]I am able to do all things through Him who strengthens me. [14]Still, you did well by sharing with me in my hardship.

[15]And you, Philippians, know that in the early days of the gospel, when I left Macedonia, no church shared with me in the matter of giving and receiving except you alone. [16]For even in Thessalonica you sent gifts for my need several times. [17]Not that I seek the gift, but I seek the fruit that is increasing to your account. [18]But I have received everything in full, and I have an abundance. I am fully supplied, having received from Epaphroditus what you provided—a fragrant offering, a welcome sacrifice, pleasing to God. [19]And my God will supply all your needs according to His riches in glory in Christ Jesus. [20]Now to our God and Father be glory forever and ever. Amen.

²¹Greet every saint in Christ Jesus. Those brothers who are with me greet you. ²²All the saints greet you, but especially those from Caesar's household. ²³The grace of the Lord Jesus Christ be with your spirit.

Philippians 4:1–23

Questions for Interaction

Leader
Refer to the Summary and Study Notes at the end of this section as needed. If 30 minutes is not enough time to answer all of the questions in this section, conclude the Bible Study by answering questions 6 and 7.

1. How do you normally respond when you are caught in the middle of a conflict?

   - ○ I try my best to avoid any uncomfortable situations.
   - ○ I am the mediator. I look to bring warring parties together.
   - ○ I get very nervous. I'm not good with conflict.
   - ○ I love a fight.
   - ○ I don't like to fight, but I will not back down.
   - ○ I will eventually win.
   - ○ Others always seem to get the best of me.
   - ○ Other _____.

2. Which of the statements in question 1 do you think represent what Paul was most like?

3. From what Paul says here what would you say is the most important key to finding personal peace?

   - ○ Rejoicing in difficult times—keeping a positive attitude (v. 4).
   - ○ Being kind and gracious to others (v. 5).
   - ○ Being confident that the Lord is always near me (v. 5).
   - ○ Maintaining a disciplined prayer life (v. 6).
   - ○ Living a moral, obedient life (vv. 8–9).
   - ○ All of the above.

4. What is Paul's secret to contentment (vv. 10–13)? How does Paul's view of contentment compare with the modern world's view of contentment?

5. What has been the most valuable thing you have learned from studying Philippians?

6. In what situation do you have the hardest time being content right now? How can what Paul says help you?

7. If you truly believed that you could do all things through Him who gives you strength, what would you attempt in the coming week?

<table>
<tr><td>**Going Deeper**</td><td>If your group has time and/or wants a challenge, go on to this question:</td></tr>
</table>

8. What is the difference between being "content" and being "complacent"? How can you be content in all circumstances without becoming complacent about some things that can and ought to be changed?

 ## Caring Time Apply the Lesson and Pray for One Another (15 minutes)

Leader
Conclude this final Caring Time by praying for each group member and asking for God's blessing in any plans to start a new group and/or continue to study together.

Gather around each other now in this final time of sharing and prayer, rejoicing in the fact that God loves you and wants you to have an abundant amount of peace and contentment in your life.

1. In what area of your life do you most need to experience the "peace of God" (v. 7) in the coming week?

2. What was the "serendipity" in your group experience—the unexpected blessing?

3. How would you like the group to continue praying for you?

Summary: Paul now pinpoints a specific problem confronting the Philippian church. Two of them, Euodia and Syntyche, have had a falling out, and their conflict is threatening the unity of the whole church. Paul identifies those attitudes that enable people to cope successfully in difficult times. Paul then goes on to thank the Philippians for a gift they had sent him, but uses the opportunity to do some more teaching.

4:2 *urge.* This is a strong verb meaning, "to exhort, to implore, to beg." The issue is so serious that Paul is willing to go on bended knee, as it were, to get it resolved. ***Euodia/Syntyche.*** Apparently these two women had carried their quarrel into the body, and it was threatening to split the church. Peace between was crucial to the unity of the whole body. ***in the Lord.*** The only hope for this kind of unity to develop between these two women is found in the fact of their common commitment to Jesus. To be "in the Lord" is to emulate the mindset of the Lord.

4:3 *true partner.* There has been much speculation about the identity of the person addressed here by Paul. He may simply be an unnamed colleague. Some suggest that the Greek word used here could be translated as if it were a proper name, *Syzygus,* in which case Paul would be reminding him to be true to his name ("true partner" or "loyal yokefellow") by assisting these women to resolve their differences.

4:4 *Rejoice.* Paul returns to this central admonition that pervades the whole epistle. This is the first of a series of attitudes that make it possible to cope successfully in a hard situation. If one is rejoicing, one cannot be despairing. Paul is not calling for people to rejoice because of the situation. Rather, it is the Lord who is the source and cause of rejoicing.

4:5 *The Lord is near.* It is possible to rejoice and to act with graciousness because the Lord will return in the very near future and bring to an end all one's trials and difficulties. The Lord is "near" in a second sense as well. He is close to His children, through the Spirit, aiding them as they face these difficulties.

4:6 *Don't worry.* This is not a command given lightly. The Philippians certainly had cause to worry, and Paul, who writes this command, is in prison. Yet to worry is to display a lack of confidence in God's care and in God's control over the situation. Jesus commands believers not to worry (Matt. 6:25–34). ***prayer/petition/requests.*** Paul uses three synonyms in a row to describe the alternative to anxiety. Instead of worrying, a person ought to converse directly with God and lay out before him all that is on his or her mind, confident that God will hear and respond.

4:7 *the peace of God.* This is the only time that this phrase is used in the New Testament. It is part of God's inner character, and also what he experiences. Amazingly, it is this peace that he offers to share with his children. ***surpasses every thought.*** Human beings can never fully understand such peace. It is the kind of peace that can never be figured out or produced by people themselves. It is that peace which relieves anxiety in a way quite beyond what people can do on their own. ***guard.*** This is a military term. It describes a garrison of soldiers, such as those stationed at Philippi, whose job it was to stand watch over the city and protect it.

4:10 *at last.* Apparently the Philippians had not been in contact with Paul for quite some time. The reason for this is not explained. However, the arrival of Epahroditus renewed their contact with Paul, for which he is grateful. *renewed.* This is a rare Greek word that appears only at this place in the New Testament. It describes the flowering of a bush or tree, and can be translated "blossomed." Paul is so grateful for their renewed care after this long silence that to him it is like seeing a shoot sprout out of the ground and burst into blossom. *You were, in fact, concerned about me.* Paul is not criticizing them for not being in touch. It is not that they did not want to come to his aid. They simply had no opportunity.

4:11 *content.* Another rare word. This is its only appearance in the New Testament. Paul tells the Philippians that he has learned to be content with whatever he has. Contentment is the virtue of bring happy with what you have and not yearning after more possessions or comforts or luxuries.

4:12 *I have learned the secret.* This is the only occurrence of this verb in the New Testament. It is used to refer to the rites by which the initiate comes to understand the secret of a cult.

4:13 *all things.* Paul is referring to what he has just described: his ability to exist in all types of material circumstances—wealth or poverty, abundant food or no food, etc. He is not suddenly making a general statement about his ability to do anything. *through Him who strengthens me.* The source of Paul's ability to exist successfully in all circumstances is his union with Christ. This is his "secret." While it is true that by going through a variety of difficult circumstances he has learned the discipline necessary to cope with hardship and abundance, it is also true that this ability is not merely self-generated. It comes from Christ.

4:16 *several times.* This is one of the few churches from which Paul has accepted multiple gifts—which is an indicator of the special relationship he has with the Philippians.

4:18 *a fragrant offering, a welcome sacrifice.* Paul now shifts his metaphor from the world of banking to the world of religion, specifically, to the idea of a sacrificial system. The gift to Paul was also a gift to God, similar to the sweet odor of animal sacrifice offered up to God.

4:21 *Those brothers.* It is not just Paul, but the ministry team he is a part of, that send greetings. Who these "brothers" are is not specified, but certainly they would include people like Timothy. This is not a reference to the church at Rome since it is mentioned in the next sentence.

4:22 *All the saints.* These are the Christians in Rome who are sending their greeting. "Saints" are all those sanctified (or made holy) by the blood of Jesus Christ, and not just those who, according to popular understanding, lived particularly pious lives. *Caesar's household.* From among the church as a whole, a particular group wishes to make known its greeting, namely those who serve on the imperial staff. This is not a reference to the actual family of Caesar. Rather, it denotes those of both high and low rank who are involved in the running of the empire. This includes soldiers, administrators, servants, high officials, etc. They are eager to meet the folk in Philippi because it is a Roman colony. Paul's use of the phrase "Caesar's household" is significant. It is an indication that Christianity had now begun to penetrate the government of the Roman Empire.

4:23 *grace.* Paul began this letter by pronouncing "grace and peace" upon the Philippians (1:2). He ends on the same note. *your spirit.* "Your" is plural and "spirit" is singular. What Paul prays is that the grace of Christ will rest on each individual believer in Philippi. The word "spirit" in this context is used to refer to the whole person, especially in his or her mental and spiritual aspects.

Personal Notes

_____

_____

_____

_____

_____

_____

_____

_____

_____

_____

_____

Personal Notes

_____

_____

_____

_____

_____

_____

_____

_____

_____

_____